A WINDOW ON WILLIAMSBURG

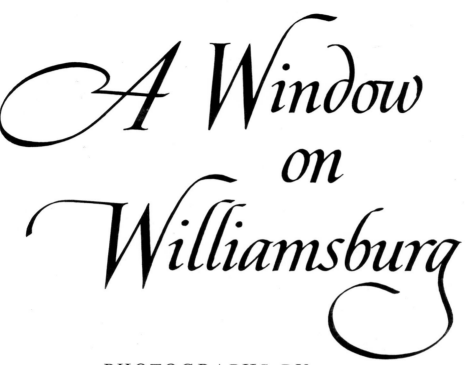

A Window on Williamsburg

PHOTOGRAPHS BY
Taylor Biggs Lewis, Jr.

TEXT BY
John J. Walklet, Jr.

COLONIAL WILLIAMSBURG
WILLIAMSBURG · VIRGINIA
Distributed by
HOLT, RINEHART AND WINSTON, INC.
New York

Library of Congress Catalogue Card Number 66-23534

SECOND PRINTING

Printed by Deeptone Offset
The Lakeside Press · R. R. Donnelley & Sons Company, Chicago, Illinois

35640

BRIGHT as the gold that lured adventurers and settlers to the new world, a dandelion thrusts its shaggy head from the embrace of gnarled paper mulberry roots in Colonial Williamsburg. Just as the dandelion seed took root in this unlikely, inhospitable spot, the seed of settlement planted more than 300 years ago on the edge of the wilderness at Jamestown by courageous Englishmen flowered into Williamsburg, capital of His Majesty's crown colony of Virginia.

Williamsburg was 77 years old when the Virginia legislators, meeting at the Capitol, defied the might of the strongest military power in the world and voted their historic Resolution for American Independence. It is this Williamsburg we see today, restored to its early appearance through the generosity of the late John D. Rockefeller, Jr., and members of his family.

A Window on Williamsburg is an intimate glimpse of the 18th-century city, its gardens and greens, its buildings great and small, its crafts, and its people.

The Elkanah Deane house and garden

Gardens are for little girls . . .
and sleepy cats . . .

and birds . . .
and hollyhocks

The
colorful
disarray . . .

of autumn
in
Williamsburg

The newly bare branches and dangling seed pods of catalpa trees form a latticework
through which are seen the last vestiges of autumn color along Palace Green

THE CAPITOL

*"What a temptation to sit in silence and let the past speak
to us of those great patriots whose voices once resounded
in these halls, and whose farseeing wisdom, high courage
and unselfish devotion to the common good will ever be an
inspiration to noble living."* —JOHN D. ROCKEFELLER, JR.

The echoes of stirring events are still heard in the Hall of the House of Burgesses at the Capitol, scene of Patrick Henry's "Caesar-Brutus" speech and his defiant Resolutions protesting the Stamp Act; George Mason's Virginia Declaration of Rights; the May 15, 1776, Resolution for Independence, which led directly to the historic July 4 decision; the pioneering Virginia Constitution of 1776, which served as a model for many other states; and the introduction of Jefferson's famous Statute for Religious Freedom

Luxury characterizes the Virginia Council Chamber in the Capitol, contrasting strongly with the austerity of the Hall of the House of Burgesses. The upper house of colonial Virginia's legislature, the Virginia Council was a non-elective body. Members were selected by the king from Virginia's landed aristocracy to serve crown and colony

The General Court at the Capitol was the highest tribunal for justice in the colony. It met twice yearly. Most of its cases were civil, but criminal offenses punishable by mutilation or death were also tried here. It was in this setting that the 15 surviving henchmen of the notorious pirate Blackbeard were brought to justice and 13 of them sentenced to be hanged for their crimes

Framed by massive candlesticks, portraits of Virginia patriots Edmund Pendleton, John Robinson, and Patrick Henry lend dignity to the Conference Room of the Capitol. It was here that members of the Virginia Council and the burgesses met to conduct morning prayer and to resolve their differences

THE GOVERNOR'S PALACE

Elizabeth I, "Good Queen Bess," a portrait c. 1585 by Marcus Geerarts the Elder in the Secretary's Office of the Capitol

"George Washington at the Battle of Trenton," by Charles Willson Peale, hangs in the hallway of the Capitol

SYMBOL of the power of the Crown in colonial Virginia, the Governor's Palace was the residence of seven royal governors, from Alexander Spotswood, the soldier-architect who supervised its building, to the tactless John Murray, Earl of Dunmore, who fled from the Palace in 1775 to the safety of a British warship in the James River, ending British rule in Virginia. The Palace also was the executive mansion for the first two governors of the commonwealth of Virginia, Patrick Henry and Thomas Jefferson

The commanding portrait of Governor Spotswood, attributed to Charles Bridges, dominates the intimate Small Dining Room of the Palace. The silver chandelier, c. 1691–97, by England's Daniel Garnier, is the only one of its kind in the United States

The Governor's Office. Every inch a man's room, its functional furnishings were selected for the comfort and convenience of the king's own representative in Williamsburg

The Large Dining Room, where guests were entertained by the royal governor
and his lady. A double-pagoda silver epergne, 1762–63, by Thomas Pitts,
English silversmith, graces the mahogany mid-18th-century dining
table. Eleven Chelsea porcelain figures, listed in the 1770 Palace inventory
of Lord Botetourt, decorate the mantel. Above hangs a portrait of King
James I, by the Italian painter Fredrigo Zuccaro, c. 1543–1609

Acoustically superb, the elegant Ballroom of the Palace still resounds
on festive occasions with sprightly airs of colonial days. The double-
keyboard harpsichord is by Jacob Kirckman, London, 1762

In the Palace Parlor, the artistry of
master cabinetmakers is evident
in the Chinese Chippendale settee
and armchair, once owned by
John Wentworth, the last royal governor
of New Hampshire

A rare silver monteith, 1710–11, made
by London craftsman Robert Cooper,
reflects the soft light of the crystal
chandelier in the Supper Room of the
Palace. The silver stand on which it rests
is also English, 1779–80

The Tudor English carved oak bed in the
Northeast Bedroom of the Palace is
adorned by hangings and spread of
English crewelwork of the period.
An oak bed was listed in the
inventory for this room

Chinese wallpaper decorates the restful
Study of the governor. The oak wing
chair, with needlework upholstery in
silk and wool, is English, c. 1700–1710;
the mahogany side chair is American,
Philadelphia, c. 1760. The governor's
desk is an English slant-top mahogany
desk, c. 1760, with brass standish
and silver candlesticks

The sophisticated tastes of 18th-century culture are evident in the
Upper Middle Room of the Palace. Spanish leather wall covering,
c. 1680, specified as "gilt Leather hangings" in a 1710 "Proposal For
rendering the new House Convenient as well as Ornamental," forms a
sumptuous backdrop for the magnificent tall case clock (*left*), c. 1699,
made by the famed clockmaker Thomas Tompion. The 17th-century
Jamaican casket on the oval oak table (*left and above*) is tortoise shell
with mother-of-pearl inlay, a gift from Britain's Queen Elizabeth II
on the occasion of her visit to Colonial Williamsburg.

Gilt gesso girandoles flank a rosewood-and-mahogany bookcase
attributed to English cabinetmaker Giles Grendy. The pier tables,
topped with Siena marble, and gilt-framed pier glasses, are also
products of English craftsmanship of the same period. Beechwood arm
chairs, with cane back and seat, a Bergama rug, cut-velvet draperies,
and an English cut-glass chandelier complete the scene

BRUTON PARISH CHURCH

Designed by Governor Spotswood, Bruton Parish Church has been in continuous use
since the days when it was the court church for the colony of Virginia. Bruton Parish was
formed in 1674 by merging two earlier parishes. The present church was completed in 1715,
and a tower was added in 1769. Church and state were united in Virginia, and
Bruton Parish represented the established church, the Anglican Church, in the colony

THE COURTHOUSE OF 1770

A symbol of law and order on Market Square for nearly two centuries,
the Courthouse was replaced in 1932 by a new structure on South England Street.
Two courts regularly met here, the James City County Court and the
municipal or hustings court. The county court was the principal agent of local
government in colonial Virginia and had broad powers, both judicial and executive

THE PUBLIC GAOL

The "strong, sweet Prison" where debtors and common criminals awaited the summary justice of the General Court. Completed in 1704, the gaol was in constant use, sometimes as a madhouse, a military prison, and later as the gaol of the city of Williamsburg until 1910

THE WREN BUILDING

The oldest academic building in English America, with its
varying roof lines, massive chimneys, and lofty cupola,
the Wren Building is the dominant feature of The College of
William and Mary yard. Its foundation was laid in 1695

THE POWDER MAGAZINE
AND GUARDHOUSE

Arms and ammunition sent to Virginia by Queen
Anne from the Tower of London were stored here.
Also designed by Governor Spotswood, the
Magazine was built in 1715

GEORGE WYTHE HOUSE

This was the home of a distinguished Virginian whose public career spanned a decisive half-century in American life. The foremost classical scholar in Virginia, George Wythe was the friend and teacher of Thomas Jefferson, a young student at The College of William and Mary who later studied law in Wythe's office and referred to him as "my faithful and beloved Mentor in youth, and my most affectionate friend through life." Wythe was executor and close friend of royal governors Fauquier and Botetourt, a burgess, speaker of the House of Delegates, a judge, the first professor of law in America at The College of William and Mary, and a signer of the Declaration of Independence

The Study

The Parlor

The Dining Room

The Student's Room

The spire of Bruton
Parish Church overlooks
Mr. Wythe's garden
and stable yard

The furnishings of the Wythe House are predominantly American. The high chest of drawers in the Northeast Bedroom (*above*) is from Boston, c. 1740. The slant-top desk was made in Rhode Island, c. 1760. In the Southwest Bedroom (*below*) all of the pieces are 18th-century American except the mahogany basin stand, English, c. 1770

RALEIGH TAVERN

This most famous of Williamsburg hostelries was dedicated to Sir Walter Raleigh, who took a leading part in sending colonists to the new world and whose leaden bust adorns the main doorway. The Raleigh was a center for social and business activity and the scene of many public auctions of land, slaves, and goods. It also ranked with the Printing Office as the postal and news center of the city

Upper left. The public dining room of the Raleigh. The early American dresser from Virginia, 1760–75, displays an outstanding collection of English and American pewter

Upper right. The famed Apollo Room, where Thomas Jefferson danced with his "fair Belinda," Rebecca Burwell, and charter members of the Phi Beta Kappa Society met regularly beneath the motto gilded above the mantel: *Hilaritas Sapientiae et Bonae Vitae Proles*— "Jollity, the offspring of wisdom and good living"

Lower left. A blazing fire adds warmth and an air of hospitality to the Raleigh taproom

BRUSH-EVERARD HOUSE

A fine example of an 18th-century house in town, this comfortable home was built in 1717 by John Brush, first keeper of the colony's Magazine on Market Square. Its most prominent owner was Thomas Everard, a gentleman of standing in the community, who was elected mayor of Williamsburg in 1766. Everard also served as auditor of Virginia and clerk of the General Court.

He was also clerk of York County from 1745 until his death in 1784.

Features of the Brush-Everard House are English ceramics in the Dining Room and the Parlor, rare moreen upholstery on the wing chair in the Parlor, and a library of 300 volumes based on a list compiled by Thomas Jefferson in 1771 for the guidance of a well-to-do planter of average intellectual interests

The Dining Room

The Northeast Bedroom

The Parlor

The Library

The Northwest Bedroom

The Child's Room

The Southwest Bedroom

The
Gardener's
Workshop

Over the rooftops
and through the fields . . . .

the unique character
of colonial Virginia
architecture . . .

becomes evident
in the homes
and in the outbuildings

Behind Waters' Storehouse and the Printing Office

Ever so briefly, winter's frosty touch
is felt throughout the city

The Greenhow-Repiton Brick Office

The St. George Tucker House

The carved horse's head at the Deane Shop and Forge, where the blacksmith labors at his anvil. Although horses were common in 18th-century Williamsburg, shoeing them was only a small part of the hammerman's job. Tidewater soil was sandy and free of stones, so most horses went unshod. But every home and farm needed some items of the ironware the smith produced—andirons, wagon tires, candle stands, and the like

The gunsmith forge-welds his gun barrels from bars of iron and carves his gunstocks from curly maple and other choice hardwoods he personally selects in the Virginia woodlands

Working with cabinet woods of the 18th century—mahogany, cherry, and walnut—the master cabinetmaker and his journeyman fashion by hand fine furniture using tools and lathes of 200 years ago

For those 18th-century colonists who could not read, the Golden Ball identified the Silversmith Shop where this master craftsman, who was usually also a jeweler, practiced his exacting trade

"Minding his P's and Q's" meant more to the colonial printer than just keeping his own counsel. It required a thorough knowledge of the type case, where his supply of hand-set type was stored. At the Printing Office on Duke of Gloucester Street, the printer once more pulls the "devil's tail" of his old hand press to produce accurate examples of early printing

In the same building, the bookbinder fashions elegant hand-tooled bindings, bookmarks, and notebooks from fine leathers and imported papers

An imposing array of elixirs and ointments, medicinal herbs, aromatic spices, and "Best Virginia" tobacco greets visitors to the Apothecary Shop. Most 18th-century apothecaries prescribed and dispensed medicines and fulfilled the role of surgeon as the occasion demanded

The trade of the perukemaker has been revived after 200 years because of the demand for high-fashion wigs. In the 18th century, however, the gentleman wore the wigs that were dressed by the wigmaker. A lady's wig, or hair, was dressed at home

The weaver at her loom in the Spinning and Weaving House where fine homespun fabrics are made in the old ways

Gingerbread men emerge from wooden molds at the bakery of the Raleigh Tavern, where breads and cakes are mixed and baked from recipes, ingredients, and equipment of colonial times

A scarecrow keeps watch over the cornfield before Robertson's Windmill, a post mill of a type well known on the Virginia peninsula in the 18th century

Unlike the horses, 18th-century citizens of Tidewater Virginia were well shod with shoes hand-sewn on wooden lasts by the bootmaker. Shoes were made with square, pointed, or round toes as fashion dictated, but most were made on straight lasts without distinction between the right and the left foot. The bootmaker also made dice cups, jewel boxes, Black Jack mugs, and other leather items to order

"Black love ribands," "Sleeve Knots,"
"Stuff Shoes for Ladies," "Cloaks and
Cardinals," such were the frills, finery, and
necessities sold by Margaret Hunter and her
sister Jane in their shop on Duke of
Gloucester Street. Here are counters once
more filled with soaps and buttons, fans,
butterfly caps and mobcaps, knitting
needles, breast flowers, and decorated
hats of Tuscan and Leghorn straw

Flax breaking

Rush seat making

Carpentry

Candle dipping and soap making

Shingle making

Transportation,

by stage . . .

a bicycle . . .

and shanks' mare

In camp, in training, or in the field, fifers and drummers were essential to 18th-century army routine. They provided the everyday sounds of a soldier's life from reveille to tattoo, improved morale and discipline, and inspired the troops in combat. Colonial Williamsburg's fifes and drums provide music of the Revolutionary period played by young musicians in authentic costume

"Balling the jack" in this case is not a 20th-century dance tune but an 18th-century game of bowls, in which off-balanced black balls are rolled at a white target ball, the "jack," by craftsmen on the Market Square green

KING'S ARMS TAVERN

In the days of William Byrd III, King's Arms was one of the most genteel taverns in the city of Williamsburg. During the Revolutionary War, its proprietress Mrs. Jane Vobe supplied food and drink to American troops, and Baron von Steuben, Prussian drillmaster of the Continental Army, was a regular patron. Today it specializes in traditional Southern foods served in the hospitable atmosphere of another age

The bountiful fare
of King's Arms

Dining by candlelight,
with service provided by
"young gentlemen of
The College of William
and Mary"

CHOWNING'S TAVERN

A typical alehouse of the colonial period, Josiah
Chowning's tavern served a less sophisticated
clientele than its famous neighbors farther down
Duke of Gloucester Street, the Raleigh and
King's Arms. Continuing in the tradition of its
early days, Chowning's serves hearty, appetizing
fare to its 20th-century patrons

A minstrel brings
a touch of gaiety
to the dinner hour

The mellow warmth of Chowning's makes each mealtime
a memorable experience

CHRISTIANA CAMPBELL'S TAVERN

was favored by George Washington and some of his friends, who had a club here. Convenient to the Capitol, this popular tavern attracted prominent leaders of the Virginia colony. Proprietress was Mrs. Christiana Campbell, described by one of her guests as "a little old woman, about four feet high; & equally thick, a little turn up Pug nose, a mouth screw'd up to one side." Today, Mrs. Campbell's Tavern once more operates in the spirit of its sprightly 18th-century hostess

Dining at Campbell's is a special treat, whether indoors or in the garden

COLONIAL WILLIAMSBURG

WILLIAMSBURG was one of the most important ideological training grounds for the leaders of American independence. For 81 influential years (1699–1780) it was the capital of the Virginia colony and a cultural and political center ranking with Boston, Newport, Philadelphia, Charleston, Annapolis, and New York. Here George Washington, Patrick Henry, George Wythe, Thomas Jefferson, George Mason, and other patriots helped shape the foundations of our government.

In 1926 Mr. John D. Rockefeller, Jr., became interested in the preservation and restoration of 18th-century Williamsburg, and thereafter devoted his personal attention and resources to the fulfillment of this goal.

The purpose of Colonial Williamsburg, in the words of the Board of Trustees, is "to re-create accurately the environment of the men and women of eighteenth-century Williamsburg and to bring about such an understanding of their lives and times that present and future generations may more vividly appreciate the contribution of these early Americans to the ideals and culture of our country."

Today, the Historic Area of Colonial Williamsburg embraces 130 acres, the heart of the old city. There are nearly 100 original 18th-century structures within this area. Several main buildings and many outbuildings that did not survive the years have been reconstructed on their original foundations after extensive archaeological investigation and historical research. Also, 90 acres of colorful gardens and greens have been recreated, using only plants known to the 18th-century colonists

DATE DUE

F			
F			
APR 19 '71			
MAR 2 '73			
OCT 3 1 '73			
F			
F			
NOV 5 '74			
FEB 26 '75			
SE 5 '80			
MR 5 '81			
NOV 1 8 '86			
JUN 1 9 '89			
AUG 08 '89			
GAYLORD			PRINTED IN U.S.A.